BRIGHT IDEA BOOKS

Dinosaurs ARE Everywhere
AND OTHER COOL JURASSIC FACTS

by Ellis M. Reed

Content Consultant

Stephanie K. Drumheller-Horton, PhD
Lecturer of Paleontology
University of Tennessee, Knoxville

CAPSTONE PRESS
a capstone imprint

Bright Idea Books are published by Capstone Press
1710 Roe Crest Drive, North Mankato, Minnesota 56003
www.mycapstone.com

Library of Congress Cataloging-in-Publication Data
Names: Reed, Ellis M., 1992- author.
Title: Dinosaurs are everywhere and other cool jurassic facts / by Ellis M. Reed.
Description: North Mankato, Minnesota : Bright Idea Books, an imprint of
   Capstone Press, [2019] | Series: Mind-blowing science facts | Audience:
   Age 9-12. | Audience: Grade 4 to 6. | Includes bibliographical references and index.
Identifiers: LCCN 2018036889 | ISBN 9781543557657 (hardcover : alk. paper) |
   ISBN 9781543557978 (ebook)
Subjects: LCSH: Dinosaurs--Juvenile literature.
Classification: LCC QE861.5 .R437 2019 | DDC 567.9--dc23
LC record available at https://lccn.loc.gov/2018036889

Editorial Credits
Editor: Meg Gaertner
Designer: Becky Daum
Production Specialist: Colleen McLaren

Photo Credits
Alamy: Xinhua, 23; iStockphoto: Elenarts, 17, fdevalera, 26–27, HomoCosmicos, 20–21, LeventKonuk, cover (foreground), USO, 18–19, Wlad74, 26; Science Source: De Agostini Picture Library, 12, Francois Gohier, 24–25; Shutterstock Images: Akkharat Jarusilawong, 11, Anurak Pongpatimet, 30–31, Herschel Hoffmeyer, 13, mgfoto, 7, mikluha_maklai, 8–9, Pavel Tvrdy, cover (background), Shvoeva Elena, 5, 15, srulik, 8

Printed in the United States of America.
PA48

TABLE OF CONTENTS

CHAPTER 1

AMAZING
Dinosaurs

Tyrannosaurus rex had a huge bite. Its thick teeth could crush bones. Velociraptor could run at least 24 miles (29 kilometers) per hour. Stegosaurus had bony plates on its back. **Dinosaurs** lived millions of years ago. They were amazing!

Stegosaurus' plates were stuck in its skin, not attached to its skeleton.

5

CHAPTER 2

DINOSAUR
Diets

Some dinosaurs ate plants. They were **herbivores**. Stegosaurus had a beak and small teeth. It ate bushes and fallen leaves or seeds. Its teeth were not very strong.

Diplodocus was 90 feet (27 meters) long. It had a long neck. It ate leaves from trees.

People can see Diplodocus skeletons in museums.

Some dinosaurs ate meat. They were **carnivores**. T. rex ate other dinosaurs. It had tiny arms. But its neck was strong. T. rex could toss **prey** in the air.

T. rex had 60 teeth, each up to 8 inches (20 centimeters) long.

Evidence from their bones shows that Velociraptors had feathers.

Velociraptor ran on two feet. Each foot had a long claw on its second toe. The dinosaur could balance on one foot. Then it slashed with the other foot. This helped it catch food.

CHAPTER 3

DINOSAUR
Defenses

Many dinosaurs had unique features. Triceratops had three horns on its head. It used these horns to fight other Triceratops. The horns might have also helped the dinosaur attract a **mate**.

Triceratops also had a large frill on the back of its head.

The ankylosaurs were a group of armored dinosaurs.

Edmontonias were ankylosaurs. They had large spikes on their necks and shoulders. They used these for **defense**. Other ankylosaurs had clubs on their tails. They used these like weapons.

THERIZINOSAURUS

One dinosaur had the longest claws in history. Its claws were about 3.2 feet (1 m) long. It used its claws to grab plants. The claws also helped with defense.

Therizinosaurus was a large dinosaur with long arms.

CHAPTER 4

DINOSAURS AND Dinosaur Cousins Today

Most dinosaur **species** are **extinct**. They do not exist anymore. But other dinosaurs are still around. Birds are dinosaurs!

Many dinosaurs were like birds.
Some had feathers. Others had hollow
bones. The bones were very light. These
dinosaurs could move quickly.

Coelophysis used
its speed to catch
small prey.

ARCHAEOPTERYX

Archaeopteryx was a dinosaur. It may also have been the first bird. It lived 150 million years ago. It had three claws on each wing. But it could not fly very well.

A BIRD WITH TEETH

Unlike today's birds, Archaeopteryx had teeth.

Archaeopteryx had wing bones similar to today's quails, birds that can fly in short bursts.

17

SHARKS

Sharks were around 420 million years ago. Some species did not become extinct. They are still alive today. But the biggest shark lived 2.6 million years ago. Megalodon was a huge shark. It hunted whales and other animals. It grew up to 59 feet (18 m) long. That is almost three times as big as today's great white shark!

Great white sharks feed on seals, sea lions, and other ocean animals.

TOOTH CLUES

Sharks' skeletons are made of **cartilage**. Cartilage rarely **fossilizes**. But scientists can study Megalodon's teeth. The teeth tell scientists how big the shark was.

Models of Sarcosuchus show its large mouth.

CROCODILES

Crocodiles lived at the same time as some dinosaurs. One crocodile was called Sarcosuchus. It was 40 feet (12 m) long. It weighed 8 tons. That is heavier than a modern African elephant! Today's saltwater crocodiles are about half this size.

BIG MOUTH

Sarcosuchus hunted on land and in water. It ate small dinosaurs. Its head was almost 6 feet (1.8 m) long!

CHAPTER 5

FINDING
Fossils

Scientists know about dinosaurs from **fossils**. Many of these are old bones. They can be millions of years old.

Scientists found a fossil in 1994. It was a small dinosaur called Citipati. The fossil was almost a complete skeleton. It was sitting on a nest of eggs.

A model of Citipati shows it near its nest.

FIGHT TO THE DEATH

Scientists once found a fossil of two dinosaurs fighting. One was a Velociraptor. Its long claw was in the other dinosaur's neck.

The other dinosaur fought back. It was a Protoceratops. Its jaws were around the Velociraptor's arm. The two dinosaurs were buried in this pose.

The fossil is known as the Fighting Dinosaurs.

Archaeopteryx fossils show traces of feathers.

Coprolite is the scientific name for fossilized poop.

Fossils can be more than dinosaur bones. There are fossils of dinosaur skin. They show some dinosaurs had scales. Other dinosaurs had feathers. There are even fossils of dinosaur poop!

GLOSSARY

carnivore
an animal that eats meat

cartilage
flexible tissue that makes up parts of animal bodies and is softer than bone

defense
self-protection

dinosaur
a member of a group of reptiles; while most of them lived millions of years ago, some still survive today as birds

extinct
no longer existing

fossil
any evidence of past life, which can include the remains of plants and animals, but also footprints, trackways, and other preserved behaviors

fossilize
to become a fossil

herbivore
an animal that eats plants

mate
an animal that is paired with another animal for making young

prey
an animal that is eaten by other animals

species
a group of animals of the same kind that can have young

TRIVIA

1. Scientists do not agree about which dinosaur was the largest. But one of the largest dinosaurs was *Patagotitan mayorum*. It was 122 feet (37 m) long. It weighed 76 tons. That is as heavy as 12 modern African elephants!

2. The smallest dinosaur ever lives today! It is the bee hummingbird. It is only about 2 inches (5 cm) long.

3. Some baby dinosaurs were eaten by snakes. The snakes were 11 feet (3.5 m) long. Scientists found fossils of these snakes next to dinosaur nests.

ACTIVITY

DINOSAUR SCIENTIST

You can be a dinosaur scientist. You can look for fossils in your own backyard! Scientists use special tools to dig for fossils. Look online to see what kinds of tools scientists use. These might include soft brushes or picks.

Then, with an adult's permission, see what you can find in your backyard. You can brush off rocks. Do they have animal footprints or tracks? You can dig into the ground. Are there bones or eggs? Look at what you find. Can you guess what kind of animal left these clues?

FURTHER RESOURCES

Love dinosaurs? Check out these resources:

Nargi, Lela. *Absolute Expert: Dinosaurs*. Washington, D.C.: National Geographic, 2018.

National Geographic Kids: Dinosaurs
https://kids.nationalgeographic.com/animals/hubs/dinosaurs-and-prehistoric/

O'Hearn, Michael. *Allosaurus vs. Brachiosaurus: Might Against Height*. North Mankato, Minn.: Capstone Press, 2010.

Wedel, Mathew J. *Totally Amazing Facts about Dinosaurs*. Mind Benders. North Mankato, Minn.: Capstone Press, 2019.

Want to know about the study of dinosaurs? Learn more here:

American Museum of Natural History: Paleontology
www.amnh.org/explore/ology/paleontology/

Holtz Jr., Thomas R. *Digging for Brachiosaurus*. Smithsonian. A Discovery Timeline. North Mankato, Minn.: Capstone Press, 2015.

INDEX